WITHDRAWN

TOP 25

BASEBALL

SKILLS, TIPS, AND TRICKS

Enslow Publishers, Inc.
40 Industrial Road
Box 398
Berkeley Heights, NJ 07922
USA

http://www.enslow.com

DAVID ARETHA

Library of Congress Cataloging-in-Publication Data

Aretha, David.
  Top 25 baseball skills, tips, and tricks / David Aretha.
      p. cm. — (Top 25 sports skills, tips, and tricks)
  Includes index.
  Summary: "Discusses baseball skills, including the basic techniques for batting, pitching, fielding, and baserunning,
and provides tips, drills, and fun tricks for young players to practice their skills"—Provided by publisher.
  ISBN 978-0-7660-3859-2
  1. Baseball—Training—Juvenile literature. I. Title. II. Title: Top twentyfive baseball skills, tips, and tricks.
  GV867.5.A73 2012
  796.357'2—dc22

                          2010044127

Paperback ISBN 978-1-59845-360-7

Printed in the United States of America

052011 Lake Book Manufacturing, Inc., Melrose Park, IL

10 9 8 7 6 5 4 3 2 1

Do not attempt the more advanced skills and tricks without adult supervision.

To Our Readers:
We have done our best to make sure all Internet addresses in this book were active and appropriate when we went to press.
However, the author and the publisher have no control over and assume no liability for the material available on those Internet
sites or on other Web sites they may link to. Any comments or suggestions can be sent by e-mail to comments@enslow.com or
to the address on the back cover.

♻ Enslow Publishers, Inc., is committed to printing our books on recycled paper. The paper in every book contains 10% to
30% post-consumer waste (PCW). The cover board on the outside of each book contains 100% PCW. Our goal is to do our part
to help young people and the environment too!

Illustration Credits: AP Images, pp. 21, 43; AP Images / Eric Gay, p. 44; AP Images / Jeff Roberson, p. 7; AP Images /
Marcio Jose Sanchez, p. 36; AP Images / Mary Butkus, p. 42; AP Images / Mike Carlson, p. 16; AP Images / Morry Gash, p. 33;
AP Images / Nick Wass, p. 19; AP Images / Ross D. Franklin, p. 23; Cathy Cesario Tardosky, p. 13; © Corbis Super RF / Alamy,
pp. 22, 39; Enslow Publishers, Inc., p. 4 (diamond diagram); Shutterstock.com, pp. 1, 4, 5, 6, 8, 9, 11, 15, 17, 20, 24–25, 27,
28, 29, 31, 34, 35, 37, 41, 45.

Cover Illustration: Shutterstock.com (Young baseball pitcher throwing to home plate).

CONTENTS

Right Fielder

Center Fielder

Second Baseman

First Baseman

Left Fielder

Shortstop

Pitcher

Third Baseman

Catcher

KNOCK THE COVER OFF THE BALL

It's your first Little League game of the season, and the coach has his eye on you. "Okay, champ," he says. "You're on deck." But are you ready?

1 BATTER UP!

Before your season begins, you need to be properly equipped. Your uniform should be neither baggy nor tight. During games, you should tuck in your jersey. For better traction when you run, wear plastic spikes instead of sneakers. Metal spikes are not allowed in Little League because of the danger they pose to opposing infielders. Also, boys should buy and wear an athletic supporter (a cup). It is highly recommended and usually required in Little League.

When you go to bat, your helmet should fit snugly. If it's too loose, it might distract you. As for your bat, it shouldn't be too heavy because then you wouldn't have a smooth swing. Also, avoid a tiny bat because you might not be able to reach balls on the outside corner of the plate. Try different bats during practice to determine which works best for you.

Practice your swing while waiting in the on-deck circle. Make sure you have the bat you want and your helmet fits snugly.

5

2 DIG IN LIKE A PRO

Let's start with the basic batting stance. First, step into the middle of the batter's box with your body facing home plate. Spread your feet several inches wider than your shoulders. Point your front foot slightly (not fully) toward the pitcher. Flex your knees and hips slightly. Tilt your body *very slightly* forward so that you have more weight on the balls of your feet (and not on your heels). If you're a right-handed hitter, lean toward your right side and put extra weight on your right foot. Keep your head level (not cocked down) with your eyes on the pitcher.

When you grip the bat, pay particular attention to how the knuckles of the top hand align with those of the bottom hand.

Grip the handle firmly with your fingers, but don't squeeze it too hard. When you're in your stance, keep the bat about six inches from your ear—with your elbows up. Your bat should not point straight up or straight back. Instead, it should be halfway in between.

Finally, before you begin your swing, gently sway your hips back and forth. You might also want to wiggle your bat. This movement will keep you loose, ready to crush the pitch.

Get a firm grip on the bat, but don't squeeze it too hard.

Head should be steady, eyes on the pitcher

Elbows high

Knees bent

Weight should be on your back foot

All-Star first baseman Albert Pujols is often called "The Machine" for his amazingly consistent hitting. The three-time National League Most Valuable Player is always prepared at the plate. You want to have a batting stance that makes you feel comfortable.

3 LET 'ER RIP!

Now it's time to drive the ball into the outfield. When the pitcher winds up, lean toward your back foot to "load" your swing. Remember to stay on the balls of your feet. Keep your eyes on the ball at all times. If you think the pitch is hittable (in the strike zone), take a full rip.

To do so, stride forward. Your front foot should move about six inches toward the pitcher. Your back foot should remain planted on the ground. Don't just swing with your arms. Move your hips forward while swinging. This allows you to put the full weight of your body into the swing. Your swing should be level—not a big uppercut. As you swing, your head should stay down, with your eyes focused on the ball.

Relax at the plate. Take a full swing, but don't try to kill the ball. As Hall of Famer Cal Ripken advised, "Concentrate on solid, hard contact."

Eyes on the ball

Swing the bat level

Rotate your hips

Only swing at a pitch if you think it's in the strike zone.

PRO TIPS AND TRICKS

Over the last fifty years, no major-leaguer has a higher career batting average than Tony Gwynn (.338). Here is his advice: "For me the most effective way to practice hitting is to use a batting tee and a bag of Wiffle balls. The sooner you hit a Wiffle ball cleanly off a tee, the sooner you will become a better hitter."

Florida Marlins shortstop Hanley Ramirez drives a ball into the outfield. Great hitting requires concentration. You don't have to hit a home run every time up—just make good contact with the baseball.

4 BE A SMART HITTER

If you want to be a great hitter, you need more than just a sweet swing. You need to be smart at the plate. First, if your third base coach has signs (for bunting, stealing, etc.), make sure you know what they are. If you are unsure what they are, ask your coach or a teammate. Before each pitch, look at the third base coach to see what sign the coach is showing.

When you're on the bench, study the opposing pitcher. Is the pitcher throwing fast or slow? Low or high? Inside or outside? Consider taking the first pitch to better determine how the pitcher is throwing.

You also need to know the game situation. Some coaches prefer you to take a 3–0 pitch in the hopes of drawing a walk. The coach may even have a "take" sign. If you have two strikes, you should concentrate on just putting the ball in play instead of taking a mighty rip (and risk striking out). "Just making contact" is also important when there's a runner on third with less than two outs. That's because the runner can score on a ground ball.

DID YOU KNOW?

About eighty years ago in Cincinnati, Ernie Lombardi belted the longest home run in history . . . sort of. Lombardi's blast cleared the center-field fence and landed in a dump truck that was driving down the road. The ball didn't stop moving until the driver finally parked his truck. By that time, the ball had traveled 30 miles—or 158,000 feet!

It's important for a hitter to develop a good "eye" at the plate. This means you'll know when to swing at a good pitch and when to hold back if a ball is off the plate.

If the coach gives you a bunt sign, this means he wants you to advance the runner. When bunting, square your body to the pitcher, and move up in the batter's box. Keep your lower hand on the bat handle, and move your upper hand to the fat part of the bat. Bunting takes a lot of practice, but it can be a great way to get on base or help your team score in a close game.

5 BATTING DRILLS

Thanks to modern technology, stars like Derek Jeter and Joe Mauer can help you with your swing. Just search "batting video" on Google or YouTube. Numerous hitting experts will show you the best way to swing a bat. Consider their advice as you practice your swing. The more you learn, the smarter you'll become as a hitter.

If you can't get to the ball field, you can still practice hitting. Many communities have batting cages, although they can be expensive. Stores sell an apparatus that is similar to tether ball: You hit the baseball and it wraps around a pole. If you can, throw a rubber ball off a big brick wall, then swing at it after it takes a bounce. Just make sure that nothing will break, such as a window!

Finally, try to take batting practice in the hours before your game. It's a surefire way to get in the groove.

THEN AND NOW

Until the 1890s, believe it or not, players were allowed to use a flat-surface bat. This came in handy when they wanted to bunt. Players used to swing heavy bats, but over time the bats became lighter with thin handles. These bats helped them generate better bat speed. Today's big-leaguers swing bats made of either ash wood or maple wood. Maple became popular in 2001 when Barry Bonds belted a record 73 home runs using maple bats.

The best way to become a great hitter is to practice. There are many drills that can help improve your swing. This coach is helping a player get ready before a game using a hitting stick. Hitting drills can be done on your own or with your friends, teammates, or coaches.

ZOOM AROUND THE BASES

Good baserunning requires smart decisions, proper technique, and lots of practice. Here are some tips to get you going.

 ## 6 GETTING ON AND GETTING A LEAD

You just cracked a shot up the middle. Now what? First of all, drop your bat—never throw it. While looking to see where you hit the ball, run as hard as you can to first base. On a ground ball to an infielder, step on the base and then fade right into foul territory.

If your hit went into the outfield, you'll need to "round the bag" at first base. Your path should be in the shape of a banana or a question mark: Run straight, then curve to the right and back to the left. Before you cross first base, look at the first base coach. The coach will either wave you to second base or put his hands up. This means you should hold at first. If it's an extra-base hit, look to the third base coach as you approach second. The coach will tell you to hold up at second or keep going to third. The coach may wave you around third for a possible home run!

Leagues have different rules for taking leads off a base. If leads are allowed in your league, get a lead of about two-and-a-half steps. If the first baseman isn't covering the bag, you can get a bigger lead. If a left-hander is pitching, watch that kid's right foot. While on the pitching rubber, a lefty is allowed to throw to first only by stepping directly toward the base. Pay attention to the pitcher until a pitch is thrown. If the pitcher throws to first, you'll need to get back to the base immediately. If you have a big lead, you may need to dive back.

When taking a lead at first, keep your knees bent and stay on the balls of your feet.

DID YOU KNOW?

On August 8, 1976, the Chicago White Sox wore shorts in a real major-league game. It was all part of a publicity stunt by owner Bill Veeck. Although bare skin made sliding painful, the White Sox beat the Kansas City Royals, 5–2.

7 THE ART OF STEALING

Leagues have different rules for stealing bases. If steals are allowed, watch your third base coach on each pitch for the steal sign. If you are stealing, take off as soon as you're sure that the pitcher will throw a pitch and not throw to first. (It is harder to steal against a lefty.) Run as hard as you can. Don't look toward the catcher, since that will slow you up. Always slide unless the third base coach tells you not to.

On pitches that get past the catcher, you should take off for second—or for third if you're on second. If you're on third and there's a wild pitch, head home only if your coach tells you to.

Base stealing is difficult to master, but it can make your team much more dangerous. All-Star outfielder Carl Crawford is one of the best base stealers in the major leagues. Crawford has tremendous speed, but he is also a smart base runner.

8 THE PERFECT SLIDE

Unless you're sure there won't be a play there, you should always slide into second base, third base, and home plate. Never slide headfirst. It is dangerous if not done properly and it's not allowed in most kids' leagues.

For the proper slide, one leg is straight and the other leg is tucked under the knee. Your hands should be up and out with the palms facing the base. Keep your head up, too.

With practice, you'll figure out when to begin the slide. (You don't want to start too early or too late.) At first, sliding might be awkward. But with proper technique and practice, your slides will become nice, smooth glides into the bag.

The proper sliding technique is important to avoid injury. Sliding can also help you reach the base safely even if the ball beats you to the bag.

9 WHAT DO YOU DO IF . . .

Whenever you are on the bases, always be alert. In baseball, there's nothing more embarrassing than wandering off the base and getting tagged out. Here is what you should do in certain situations:

- If you're on first and the batter hits a grounder, always run to second immediately.

- If you're on second and the batter hits a grounder to first or second, run to third. If you're on second and the hitter grounds to the shortstop or third, stay on second unless the coach tells you to go to third.

- If the ball is hit with two outs—even in the air—always run immediately. Watch your third base coach for further instructions.

- If the batter hits the ball in the air with zero or one outs, take a short lead from your base. If the fielder catches it, you have to go back to the bag.

- If a fly ball is hit deep enough, you can tag up. Suppose you're on third base and the batter flies out to center field. After the fielder catches the ball, you can try to score from third. However, you must have a foot on third base when or after the outfielder catches the ball.

During the game, you will find yourself in many different situations on the base paths. Always pay attention to your coaches. The more experience you get, the better you'll be.

Cal Ripken, Jr., played in 2,632 consecutive games, a major-league record, before retiring in 2001. The "Iron Man" also knew a thing or two about baserunning. In this photo, he avoids the tag of Chicago White Sox first baseman Frank Thomas on July 19, 1997.

PRO TIPS AND TRICKS

On his Web site, Baltimore Orioles Hall of Famer Cal Ripken, Jr., talks about the importance of a secondary lead: "On every pitch, you should generate momentum towards the next base in a secondary lead. Think of shuffling with three hops and count them in your head—one, two, three. As the pitcher delivers the ball to the plate, you begin advancing towards the next base in the form of those three hops. You want your feet to come down on 'three' just as the ball enters the strike zone."

10 BASERUNNING DRILLS

Do you or your friends have a Slip 'n Slide? If so, it's the perfect way to practice your baseball slide. You can't get a skin burn, and it's so much fun! Some coaches suggest sliding on wet grass, although that could lead to some nasty pant stains. Stores offer sliding pants, made exclusively for sliding. Large sliding mats are another option.

At the ball field, you can practice baserunning with your teammates or friends. If you're on first and your buddy singles, try to go to third. On a fly ball, tag up and run to the next base. You need just three kids to practice leads—a pitcher, a first baseman, and a base runner at first base. The pitcher throws to first, and the runner responds accordingly. The runner also can practice getting good jumps for steals.

Practice baserunning drills with your friends and teammates. That way, when the dust settles, you'll be safe at the bag!

The legendary Ty Cobb studied pitchers to learn when they would throw home or throw to first base, but he had to do it during live games. Today's technology allows the great base stealers to watch videos of pitchers to gain an edge on the base paths.

THEN AND NOW

A hundred years ago, base-stealing great Ty Cobb used to kick first base an inch or two toward second base—which was possible to do back then. It allowed him to be closer to second base when he tried to steal. Today, baseball's great base stealers study videos of each pitcher. They try to find the exact moment when they're sure the pitcher will deliver a pitch and not throw to first. That's when they'll take off.

BLOW IT BY 'EM

It can be scary and lonely on the pitcher's mound, especially if you're not sure what to do. But you'll be a pitching ace (and not a disgrace!) if you follow this pitching advice.

11 LET'S START WITH THE RULES

When you pitch, your foot has to be touching the pitching rubber. Once you begin your pitch, you cannot stop. If you are

right-handed, you will want to throw to first or second base to keep the runner close to the bag. To do so, you have to step off the mound before you throw there. If you're right-handed and want to throw to third, you don't have to step off the mound. However, you do have to point your left leg directly at third when you throw to that base. Balks don't exist in Little League.

A lot of pitching is preparation. Know your best pitches and the locations you like to throw them to. Pitching often depends on the situation, so listen to your coaches and be aware of everything going on during the game.

However, an umpire might penalize you for breaking these rules by awarding the batter a "ball."

As you advance in baseball, the pitching rules become more complicated. You'll need to learn the difference between "pitching out of a stretch" and pitching from a windup. (You can pitch from a windup only if no one is on base.) You also will need to understand the complicated balk rule. If you are serious about pitching, discuss these rules with your coach or a former pitcher.

Tim Lincecum is nicknamed "The Freak." He led the National League in strikeouts in 2008, 2009, and 2010. But before you can pitch like this superstar, you must learn the rules.

12 AND HERE'S THE PITCH . . .

Your Little League coach probably wants you to pitch out of the stretch at all times. If you are right-handed, stand with your right foot against the rubber. Hold the ball in the glove with your hands below your chest. Your left shoulder should point toward home plate. Begin your motion by lifting your left knee up to waist level. (Your left foot should naturally hover around your right knee.) At the same time, pull the ball behind you (toward second base). Lean back on your right leg.

As you throw, take a long stride forward with your left foot. Rotate your right hip toward the plate. Keep your right elbow high. At the release, "push" the ball with your body. Snap your

wrist down and through. Your arm should follow through until the back of your right shoulder faces the plate. Remember to focus on the catcher's mitt. Try for a smooth, easy motion. You don't want to strain your arm.

Those are the basics. You will need to work with your coach to fine-tune your pitching motion. After that, you'll need to practice, practice, practice.

It is important to repeat your pitching motion the same way each time. This will help develop your control. When you can repeat the same motion over and over again, you will be able to hit the corners of the plate with your pitches much more often.

13 PREPARE FOR THE CHALLENGE

Pitching can be exciting—and nerve-racking. You'll want to prepare yourself physically and mentally. Always stretch out before the game to keep yourself limber. Briefly practice pitching early in the day to get in the groove. Also, throw from the mound or with a catcher just prior to the game.

When you're on the mound, relax. Take deep breaths and think calming thoughts. Think about your proper pitching mechanics and focus on the catcher's glove.

Early in your pitching "career," just try to throw strikes. As you get older, work on throwing on the inside and outside corners. You'll usually want to keep the ball low in order to induce harmless ground balls. However, you can pitch high on occasion to surprise the hitter. Changing speeds also throws hitters off balance. You should not throw breaking balls in Little League, because it could damage your arm.

PRO TIPS AND TRICKS

Hall of Famer Nolan Ryan remains the only pitcher to strike out 5,000 big-league batters. How did he do it? Largely through the power of concentration. He wrote: "I just block things out, focusing completely on the task of retiring the hitter. . . . [N]othing else in the world exists but the catcher's target, the hitter, and my perfect delivery. This is a space where I feel comfortable and relaxed. I don't get distracted by all the external stuff going on around me."

The basic grips for the two-seam fastball (left) and four-seam fastball are shown here. As you begin pitching, learn to throw these pitches for strikes. Pitching is all about location. Even if you can throw really hard, it won't matter if you cannot find the strike zone.

14 FIELDING YOUR POSITION

As a pitcher, you have responsibilities beyond throwing to hitters. If leads are allowed in your league, you'll want to throw to the bases to make sure runners don't get a big lead. On a ground ball to the first baseman, run to first base to take the throw and tag the bag. If your pitch gets past the catcher and the runner on third rushes home, you need to race to the plate to take the catcher's throw.

While it is very important to practice pitching, you must also rest your arm. The pitching motion puts a lot of strain on your arm, and it needs rest to avoid injury.

THEN AND NOW

In 1884, Old Hoss Radbourn won 59 games while pitching 678 innings. Today, coaches are very concerned about pitch counts, from Little League to the majors. They don't want to ruin their pitchers' arms. Nowadays, a big-league manager usually won't let his closer pitch more than one inning in a game. Even in Little League, a pitcher is only allowed to throw a certain amount of pitches per game, or innings per week.

15 PITCHING DRILLS

Even if you live in Alaska, you can practice your pitching form any day of the year. On a regular basis, practice the proper motions in your home. Study the numerous pitching videos that are online. Coaches and big-leaguers will give you an endless amount of valuable advice.

You can practice pitching on your own with a Pitch Back or something similar. The Pitch Back includes a net with a strike zone, and the pitch bounces back to you. Make sure that your homemade pitching rubber is 46 feet from your target. That's the distance between the rubber and the plate in Little League. Practice pitching as much as you can throughout the year without straining your arm. "Muscle memory" is a key to success.

Pedro Martinez throws a pitch during the 2009 World Series for the Philadelphia Phillies. Martinez gets terrific movement on his fastball and throws a great change-up.

THE ART OF DEFENSE

It's easy to call "I got it!" But it's not so easy to get it. These tips will help you fine-tune your defensive skills.

16 SCOOPING UP GROUNDERS

Baseball is a slow-moving game, but infielders need to be on high alert. As the pitcher begins to throw, get ready. Spread your legs slightly, crouch down, and lean forward on the balls of your feet. You need to be ready to move in every direction.

If a ground ball is hit slowly to you, charge in for it. If it's hit hard to your right or left, bolt immediately in that direction. You want the ball to be in front of your body when you field it—not at your side. As you go to field the ground ball, crouch low. Keep your mitt very low and in front of you. With your eyes, follow the path of the ball into your mitt. With your glove (and your free hand next to the glove), scoop the ball up toward the middle of your body.

Stand up straight and throw to the proper base. Step toward your target (the fielder's glove) and fire the ball overhand (not sidearm). You'll throw with more control if you have your index and middle fingers on the seam of the ball.

PRO TIPS AND TRICKS

New York Mets All-Star David Wright offers this tip for fielding ground balls: "Pretend that you have an eye in your glove. . . . You want to keep that eye right on the ball. When you're approaching the ball, this eye has to see the ball in order to catch it. Once you do catch it . . . cradle it into your body so that you can prepare to throw."

Use your opposite hand to help trap ball in glove

Knees bent so you can crouch low

Keep glove low and in front of you

When playing any infield position, there is not much reaction time. You must be ready at all times for the ball to be hit your way. Stay focused on the game or you might let one go through your legs!

17 I'VE GOT IT!

In Little League, most balls hit into the outfield are not caught. But you can be a hero. If the fly ball is hit away from you, run hard toward the direction of the ball. It is hard to catch the ball while running, so if you can, try to be there waiting for it. Catch the ball "with two hands," meaning use your bare hand to steady the glove.

Normally, you'll throw the ball to the cut-off person. Sometimes, however, it's smart to throw directly to a base if you think you can get a runner out.

DID YOU KNOW?

You don't need a brand-new glove to be a good fielder. Pittsburgh Pirates second baseman Bill Mazeroski was known for using old, beat-up gloves. He felt comfortable with them, and they helped him win eight Gold Glove Awards. One of Mazeroski's gloves was so beat up that teammate Roberto Clemente tossed the mitt into the stands. A kid took one look at the patched-up "piece of junk" and threw it back on the field!

Use your bare hand to steady your glove.

Even the pros follow the fundamentals of catching a fly ball. Ichiro Suzuki, an outfielder for the Seattle Mariners, has won nine Gold Gloves. In this photo, Ichiro slides to make a catch, demonstrating the "two-hand" method.

18 HE'S GOING!

This is what the infielders should do in certain situations:

- Unless it's a force-out situation, you always have to tag the runner to get that player out.

- If a runner is trying to steal second base, the second baseman should cover if a right-handed hitter is batting. The shortstop should cover if a lefty is up.

- On a ground ball to short or third with a runner on first, the second baseman covers second. On a grounder to first or second with a runner on first, the shortstop covers second.

- If leads are allowed, the first baseman should hold the runner on—then return to position once the pitch is thrown.

- On a base hit to the right side of the outfield, the second baseman should go out and take the cut-off throw from the outfielder. The shortstop handles the other side of the outfield.

Your coaches will go over other situations with you. They include double plays, bunt plays, and what to do when a runner is on third. They also include pulling the infielders in, guarding the lines, and backing up your fellow infielders.

You just caught the ball. Where should you throw it to? How many outs are there? It's important to always know the game situation so you know what to do when the ball is hit to you.

Boston Red Sox first baseman Kevin Youkilis stretches to catch a throw. The first baseman must hold runners at first and then get back into position once the pitch is thrown.

19 TAKING CHARGE BEHIND THE PLATE

As a catcher, you are involved in every play. You also get to wear cool stuff! If a pitcher throws hard, wear a batting glove under your catcher's mitt.

Squat behind home plate, standing on the balls of your feet. If you are right-handed, keep your left foot slightly ahead of the right. Hold your glove low (and steady) in the strike zone to give the pitcher a good target. Keep your free hand in a fist behind your back to avoid injury. On a pitch in the dirt, do your best to block it. Your body should be like a wall, so that if the ball caroms off you it will stay in front of you.

San Francisco Giants catcher Bengie Molina tags out a runner at home plate. Although catcher is a tough position, the Molina family has made a great living out of it. Not only is Bengie a major-league catcher, but his brothers Yadier and Jose are, too. All three have won World Series championships.

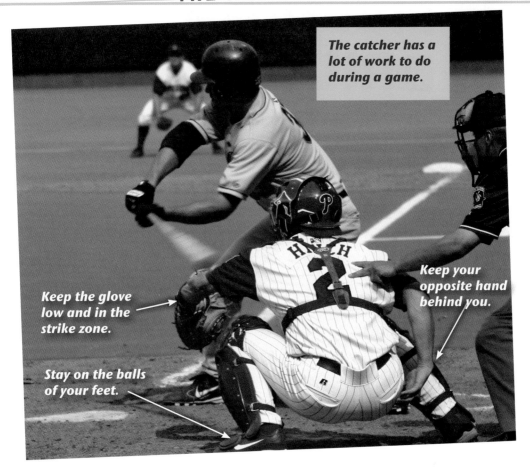

The catcher has a lot of work to do during a game.

Keep the glove low and in the strike zone.

Stay on the balls of your feet.

Keep your opposite hand behind you.

Encourage your pitcher, and always make a good throw back to him or her. On pop-ups, throw off your helmet so you can see better. Do the same for little hits in front of the plate or balls that get past you. On plays at the plate that are not force plays, stand around the plate when you catch the ball. Hold it tightly and tag the runner out.

If a runner is stealing, concentrate first on catching the ball. Don't interfere with the batter's swing—someone could get hurt. Deliver a strong throw to the base. Don't throw if you think you have no chance of getting the runner out.

20 FIELDING DRILLS

Whenever you arrive at the ball field, the first thing you should do (after stretching) is play catch. Start from a short distance and keep moving back. This helps you maintain your accuracy while increasing the strength of your throws.

To practice fielding, have someone hit or throw ground balls to you. Concentrate on proper technique. You can even field ground balls on your own by throwing a tennis ball off a brick wall. While playing 500 with your buddies, practice the proper jump and route to the fly ball. If someone is hitting grounders on the diamond, work on various situations: "There's a runner on first. Turn a double play." The possibilities for practice—and fun—are endless.

THEN AND NOW

Until the late 1800s, no player except the catcher wore gloves. Second baseman Bid McPhee was the last bare-handed fielder in the major leagues. He retired in 1899. Today's gloves have deeper pockets, making it easier to catch the ball. Companies make gloves for infield, first base, outfield, and, of course, catcher. Today, a good glove can cost more than $200.

The game 500 can be a fun way to practice catching fly balls.
Not only do you get better at tracking the flight of the ball,
but you also might need to out-jump your friends to catch it.

HOW THE BIG-LEAGUERS DO IT

Grab a Ping-Pong paddle and twist like a tornado! You can learn some interesting and unusual tips when you read about the major-leaguers.

21 HALL OF FAME WISDOM

These Baseball Hall of Famers have some advice for you:

Wee Willie Keeler: "Hit 'em where they ain't." (Hit the ball where the fielders aren't.)

Warren Spahn: "Hitting is timing. Pitching is upsetting timing."

Ted Williams (as retold by fellow Hall of Famer George Kell): "When that pitcher throws your pitch, the one you've been looking for, you don't take, you don't miss it, you don't foul it off. You hit it, and you hit it hard."

Finally, you should always have fun. As Hall of Fame slugger Willie Stargell said, "When they start the game, they don't yell, 'Work ball!' They say, 'Play ball!'"

PRO TIPS AND TRICKS

Hall of Famer Rod Carew became an outstanding bunter through hours and hours of practice. His trick was to lay handkerchiefs on the infield. He would then try to bunt balls on or near the hankies. Give it a try!

Remember, baseball is a game. So when you're out there, have fun!

22 THE BIG-LEAGUE BAG OF TRICKS

Over the years, players have come up with creative ways to improve their craft. Craig Biggio worked to become a Gold Glove second baseman by fielding grounders with a Ping-Pong paddle instead of a glove. Hall of Fame pitcher Steve Carlton put cotton in his ears to drown out the crowd noise. In addition, he strengthened his arm by swirling it in a vat of rice.

As a kid, Ozzie Smith used to throw the ball high over his house and then run to the backyard to catch it. He never succeeded, but such determination helped him become a Hall of Fame shortstop.

St. Louis Cardinals shortstop Ozzie Smith leaps in the air to turn a double play on July 28, 1996. Smith was an outstanding shortstop.

DID YOU KNOW?

According to legend, Negro League pitcher Satchel Paige threw fifty-five no-hitters. He fired a variety of different pitches, and he gave each one a silly name. His pitch nicknames included "Bat Dodger," "Hurry-up Ball," "Two-hump Blooper," and "Barber." According to legend, the "Barber" ball shaved the hairs off the batter's chin!

23 MY, HOW THE GAME HAS CHANGED!

In the big leagues, the approach to offense has changed over the years. In the early 1900s, teams used "small ball" tactics such as bunting. In the 1920s, Babe Ruth ushered in the era of the home run. In the 1960s to 1980s, the stolen base became a weapon. (In 1982, Rickey Henderson of the Oakland A's stole 130 bases!) Hitting became a science under such batting "professors" as Charlie Lau and Walt Hriniak. Today's teams analyze videos of swings and pitching to get an edge.

Nevertheless, it is still the same, simple, wonderful game it has always been: batter versus pitcher, three outs per inning, nine innings per game.

Babe Ruth belts a home run into the upper deck at Yankee Stadium in 1927. The "Great Bambino" hit sixty home runs that season. Ruth was major-league baseball's first big-time home run hitter.

24 HEY, WHATEVER WORKS . . .

Once you master the proper batting stance, feel free to experiment a little. Hall of Famer Joe Morgan used to flap his back arm before pitches. Slugger Willie Stargell twirled his bat in circles, and Craig Counsell raised his bat to the heavens.

Some pitchers have employed unusual windups. Juan Marichal's leg kick was so high, his foot pointed to the clouds. Luis Tiant twisted around toward center field before delivering. Hideo Nomo was nicknamed the "Tornado" for his twirling, explosive windup.

As a pitcher or a hitter, you need to do what makes you feel comfortable. Some major-league stars have developed unusual mechanics. Hideo Nomo was nicknamed the "Tornado" for his twirling, twisting windup and delivery.

THEN AND NOW

Today's major-league players make an average of $3 million a year. However, we can learn some lessons of humility from the stars of yesteryear. In 1971, the Detroit Tigers offered All-Star outfielder Al Kaline a salary of $100,000, but he turned it down. "I hadn't come off a good enough year to deserve the tremendous honor of a six-figure salary," Kaline said. "So I refused."

25 BE SMART AND STAY ALERT

In 1990, Steve Lyons of the Chicago White Sox slid into first base. That was strange enough. But then, to clean out the dirt, he pulled his pants down. Suddenly, he realized that he wasn't alone. Thousands of people were watching. He was so embarrassed.

The moral of the story: Always keep your head in the game. Be alert. Know how many outs there are. When you're batting, know what the count is. As a fielder, think about what to do if the ball is hit to you. Finally, and most importantly, always keep your pants on!

Baseball is a team game. Always be prepared, stay alert, and keep your focus during the game. You want to do your part for the team. When the game is over, you can celebrate with your teammates.

GLOSSARY

★**balk**—An illegal motion or action by the pitcher. As a penalty, runners are allowed to advance one base.

★**closer**—The pitcher who is often used to finish the game.

★**cut-off person**—The infielder who goes into the outfield to take the throw from the outfielder.

★**force-out**—A situation where the runner is put out when forced by the batter to move to the next base and when a fielder with the ball touches that base first.

★**Gold Glove Award**—Presented to the best fielder at each position in the National and American leagues.

★**lead**—The distance from the base that a base runner takes before each pitch.

★**"muscle memory"**—After practicing many, many times, the body's muscles "remember" what to do.

★**pitching out of the stretch**—The pitcher begins the pitch while facing first or third base and with the side of his or her foot against the pitching rubber.

★**secondary lead**—A longer lead taken by the runner after the pitch is thrown.

★**strike zone**—The area in which the umpire will call a strike. The strike zone is over home plate and between the knees and chest of the batter.

★**tag up**—The base runner goes to the next base after a fly ball is caught.

★**"take" sign**—An order by the coach to the hitter. The sign means don't swing at the next pitch.

46

FURTHER READING

Books

Doeden, Matt. *The World's Greatest Baseball Players*. Mankato, Minn.: Capstone Press, 2010.

Dreier, David. *Baseball: How It Works*. Mankato, Minn.: Capstone Press, 2010.

Jacobs, Greg. *The Everything Kids' Baseball Book: Today's Superstars, Great Teams, Legends—and Tips on Playing Like a Pro!* Cincinnati, Ohio: Adams Media, 2006.

Kelley, James E. *Baseball: Discover the History, Heroes, Gear and Games of America's National Pastime*. New York: DK Children's, 2010.

Krasner, Steven. *Play Ball Like the Hall of Famers: Tips for Kids From 19 Baseball Greats*. Atlanta, Ga.: Peachtree, 2005.

Pellowski, Michael J. *The Little Giant Book of Baseball Facts*. New York: Sterling, 2007.

Internet Addresses

MLB.com: Kids Club
<http://www.mlb.com/mlb/kids>

National Baseball Hall of Fame and Museum
<www.baseballhall.org>

Weplay: Youth Baseball Drills & Skills
<http://www.weplay.com/youth-baseball/drills>

INDEX